First Facts

First Cookbooks

A Princess COOKBOOK

Simple Recipes for Kids

by Sarah L. Schuette

CAPSTONE PRESS
a capstone imprint

First Facts is published by Capstone Press,
151 Good Counsel Drive, P.O. Box 669, Mankato, Minnesota 56002.
www.capstonepub.com

 Books published by Capstone Press are manufactured with paper
containing at least 10 percent post-consumer waste.

Library of Congress Cataloging-in-Publication Data
Schuette, Sarah L., 1976-
  A princess cookbook : simple recipes for kids / by Sarah L. Schuette.
      p. cm.—(First facts. First cookbooks)
  Summary: "Provides instructions and close-up step photos for making a variety of simple snacks and
drinks with a princess theme"—Provided by publisher.
  Includes bibliographical references and index.
  ISBN 978-1-4296-5374-9 (library binding)
  1. Cooking—Juvenile literature. I. Title. II. Series.

  TX652.5.S3438 2011
  641.5'123—dc22

                          2010028138

Editorial Credits
Lori Shores, editor; Juliette Peters, designer; Sarah Schuette, photo stylist; Marcy Morin,
      studio scheduler; Laura Manthe, production specialist

Photo Credits
All photos by Capstone Studio/Karon Dubke

The author dedicates this book to her goddaughter, Muriel Hilgers.

Printed in the United States of America in North Mankato, Minnesota.
092010
005933CGS11

Table of Contents

Royal Recipes

Every day is special when you treat yourself like a princess. Spoil yourself and **dazzle** your friends with these royal and tasty treats. Just dance your way into the royal kitchen and cook up some fun!

Princesses like to plan ahead. Read over your recipes. Look for the **ingredients** you will need. Ask an adult if you have questions. And remember, a clean princess is a pretty princess. Make sure to wash your hands before you begin. Then pick up your **palace** when you're finished.

Metric Conversion Chart	
United States	**Metric**
¼ teaspoon	1.2 mL
½ teaspoon	2.5 mL
1 teaspoon	5 mL
1 tablespoon	15 mL
¼ cup	60 mL
⅓ cup	80 mL
½ cup	120 mL
⅔ cup	160 mL
¾ cup	175 mL
1 cup	240 mL
1 ounce	30 gms

Tools

Princesses need more than crowns and ball gowns to make delicious treats. Use this handy guide to find the tools you need.

cookie cutter—a hollow shape made from metal or plastic that is used to cut cookie dough

ice cream scoop—a kitchen tool with a deep, round end for scooping ice cream

liquid measuring cup—a glass or plastic measuring cup with a spout for pouring

measuring cups—round, flat cups with handles used for measuring dry ingredients

measuring spoons—spoons with small deep scoops used to measure both wet and dry ingredients

mixing bowl—a sturdy bowl used for mixing ingredients

Techniques

measure—to take a specific amount of something

shake—to move quickly back and forth or up and down

spread—to cover a surface with something

sprinkle—to scatter something in small drops or bits

thaw—to bring to room temperature from frozen

toss—to mix gently with two spoons or forks

Magic Wands

Poof! A fairy godmother uses a magic wand to make
a princess' wish come true. What's your secret wish?
Wave these pretty pretzel wands and see what happens. **Makes 10 wands**

Ingredients:
- 1 can whipped frosting, 16 ounces
- 10 large pretzel sticks
- colored sugar sprinkles

Tools:
- wax paper
- spoon

1 Take lid and foil wrapper off a can of frosting.

2 Lay a piece of wax paper on the table to work on.

3 Use a spoon to spread frosting on the pretzel sticks. Leave some space uncovered at one end for holding the wands.

4 Sprinkle colored sugar over the frosted pretzel sticks.

5 Let wands dry on the wax paper for 10 minutes.

Royal Jewels

A princess would never go out without her jewels. You'll be the belle of the ball wearing these sweet pieces. Use different candies to match your ball gown and dance the night away in style.

Makes 1 bracelet

Ingredients:
- ½ cup colorful cereal with holes in the middle
- ½ cup candy with holes in the middle
- 1 licorice string

Tools:
- measuring cups
- 2 small bowls

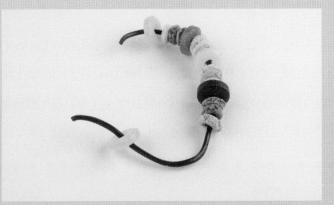

1 Measure cereal and candy and put in separate bowls.

2 Thread cereal and candy pieces on licorice string. Add cereal and candy pieces until there is enough to fit around your wrist.

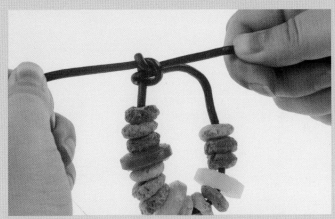

3 Tie the ends of the licorice string together. Be sure to leave enough room to fit your wrist through the bracelet.

TIP Make a matching necklace by tying more licorice strings together.

Fairy-Tale Floats

One sip and these fizzy treats will have you floating off to fairy-tale land. Daydream about living happily ever after in your own **castle**. After all, anything is possible in your own fairy tale!

Makes 2 drinks

Ingredients:

- 1 pint non-fat frozen yogurt
- 1 bottle of diet lemon-lime soda, 20 ounces

Tools:

- liquid measuring cup
- 2 glasses
- ice cream scoop
- 2 straws
- 2 spoons

1 Place frozen yogurt on counter for two minutes to thaw.

2 Measure and pour ¼ cup of soda into each glass.

3 Add two scoops of frozen yogurt to each glass.

4 When the fizzing stops, pour more soda to fill the glasses.

5 Add a straw and a spoon to each glass.

TIP Make princess pops by freezing the float mixture in an ice cube tray.

Princess and the Pea Salad

You don't have to put peas under your mattress to prove you're a princess. Just toss up this sweet salad and give the royal family a treat.

Makes 4 servings

Ingredients:

- ½ cup fat-free mayonnaise
- 1 tablespoon sugar
- 1 tablespoon vinegar
- ¼ cup milk
- 1 bag of lettuce pieces, washed
- 2 cups frozen peas, thawed
- ½ cup shredded cheese
- ⅛ cup bacon bits
- 20 small tomatoes

Tools:

- measuring cups
- measuring spoons
- liquid measuring cup
- large bowl
- spoon
- 2 forks

1 Measure and pour mayonnaise, sugar, vinegar, and milk into a large bowl. Stir with a spoon.

2 Add the lettuce and peas to the bowl.

3 Measure and add shredded cheese and bacon bits to the bowl.

4 Put the small tomatoes in the bowl.

TIP Add 1 cup of chopped cauliflower for a tasty addition.

5 Use two forks to gently toss the salad together.

Slipper Sandwiches

Cinderella lost her glass slipper when she ran home from the ball. These slipper sandwiches are so good, even Cinderella wouldn't leave one behind.

Makes 1 sandwich

Ingredients:

- 2 slices of whole grain bread
- 1 tablespoon whipped cream cheese
- 1 tablespoon strawberry jam

Tools:

- plate
- measuring spoons
- shoe-shaped cookie cutter

1 Place two slices of whole grain bread on a plate.

2 Measure cream cheese. Use the measuring spoon to spread it on one slice of bread.

3 Measure and spread jam on top of the cream cheese.

4 Put the slices of bread together with the cream cheese and jam inside.

5 Use a cookie cutter to cut out a shoe shape. Save the rest of the sandwich for later.

TIP These slipper sandwiches are still a treat when made with peanut butter and jelly.

Castle Crunch

Tucked away in her castle, Sleeping Beauty slept for many years. When she woke up, she was hungry! This snack would have been a sweet treat after a long sleep.

Makes 6 servings

Ingredients:

- ½ cup dried cranberries
- ½ cup banana chips
- ½ cup peanuts
- 1 cup cereal with colorful marshmallows

Tools:

- measuring cups
- large mixing bowl
- plastic wrap
- large spoon
- 6 paper cups

1 Measure and pour cranberries, banana chips, peanuts, and cereal into a large mixing bowl.

2 Cover the bowl with plastic wrap. Shake the bowl gently to mix ingredients.

3 Use a large spoon to put mixture into six paper cups.

Princess Parfait

Guests to Rapunzel's tower had to climb up her long braids to visit. If she had served these pink **parfaits**, they wouldn't have minded the climb.

Makes 1 parfait

Ingredients:
- 1 cup raspberries
- 6-ounce container of raspberry yogurt
- ½ cup granola

Tools:
- tall glass
- spoon
- measuring cups
- measuring spoons

TIP

Yogurt is part of the dairy food group. Eating dairy helps keep your teeth and bones strong.

1 Put three raspberries in a tall glass.

2 Put two spoonfuls of yogurt on top of the raspberries.

3 Sprinkle a little granola on top of the yogurt.

4 Repeat steps 1 through 3 to layer fruit, yogurt, and granola in the glass.

Glossary

castle (KASS-uhl)—a large building or home often surrounded by a wall and water

dazzle (DAZ-uhl)—to amaze someone

ingredient (in-GREE-dee-uhnt)—an item used to make something else

palace (PAL-iss)—a large, grand home for a king, queen, or other ruler

parfait (par-FAY)—a cold dessert made by layering different foods in a tall, narrow glass

technique (tek-NEEK)—a method or way of doing a certain skill

Read More

Beery, Barbara. *Pink Princess Cookbook.* Salt Lake City, Utah: Gibbs Smith, 2006.

Fauchald, Nick. *Holy Guacamole!: and other Scrumptious Snacks.* Kids Dish. Minneapolis, Minn.: Picture Window Books, 2008.

Wilkes, Angela. *First Cooking Activity Book.* London: Dorling Kindersley, 2008.

Internet Sites

FactHound offers a safe, fun way to find Internet sites related to this book. All of the sites on FactHound have been researched by our staff.

Here's all you do:

Visit *www.facthound.com*

Type in this code: 9781429653749

Super-cool stuff! Check out projects, games and lots more at www.capstonekids.com

Index